Are You Dancing

in the Rain?

Rain comes along,
but don't lose heart

Life Is A Matter of Choices

Cyril Prabhu

Are You Dancing in the Rain?
ISBN: 978-0-692-18967-2
Copyright © 2012 Cyril Prabhu
Reprinted 2018

Published by Blesspatt Books
Charlotte, NC – USA

DEDICATION

This book is dedicated to
single moms everywhere.

CONTENTS

INTRODUCTION

We all have memories from our childhood days that we would love to relive. Some are very comforting, and most we cherish. As we grow older, our hearts get lighter as we reminisce. Childhood memories may even make you feel younger, and they can have a lasting impact.

One such memory embedded in my mind is of  playing in the rain which were some of my most carefree and enjoyable moments! If only God could give us a chance to go back and relive those moments with the same innocence, how wonderful that would be.

As we get older and mature, dancing in the rain refreshes our souls and melts away our worries as the cooling drops of moisture splatter across our faces. If you grew up in a rural area, you will remember the fresh scent of the wet earth.

Throughout life, we encounter bumps and turns in the road that challenge the resilience of our mental strength.

Every one of us dances…

At times, our dance is not perfect because we are missing beats, or we lack the strength to sway and step with the same zeal and energy.

At those moments in life, we long for guidance and help from people who have found their rhythms in the midst of the rain. Motivational Author Vivian Greene once said, "Life's not about waiting for

the storms to pass…It's about learning to dance in the rain."

While there are differences in our dance, throughout this book, I will walk you through dance lessons learned by a young boy raised by a single mom in a metropolitan city in India. Faced with real big-city challenges, he learns to constantly adjust. But as we explore his journey's perils and triumphs, don't be surprised by the kindness of people who appear only for a season to teach him how to dance with love and affection in the middle of a downpour.

Even as a young man, he earnestly searches for answers to age-old questions like, "Why can I not find stamina to bounce back and dance when things fall apart?"

Nothing ever goes away until it has taught us what we need to know.

But as time progresses, he catches sobering glimpses of his life, forcing him to realize his quests were hidden in events he was trying to decipher in isolation.

As he channels his energy toward the positive aspects of life, the rhythm in his dance gets better and better each day. He begins to appreciate his mysterious life surrounded by beautiful and kind-hearted people who love selflessly, expecting nothing in return.

Such radical self-realizations reignite his faith, his belief system and his compassion for life. He comes to realize that dreams and aspirations are nurtured when we seek to grow during trials while gleaning from our inspirational role models.

While exploring the basis for his own existence, he is transformed as mysteries concealed in his own heart are revealed.

The Story of My Existence

That's right! It is a story about my life's journey surrounded by strong currents of challenge, relief and blessings beautifully orchestrated by God.

The Hebrew-Christian Bible repeatedly stresses the Father's love. We see a great example of this in the love Jacob, the Bible patriarch, had

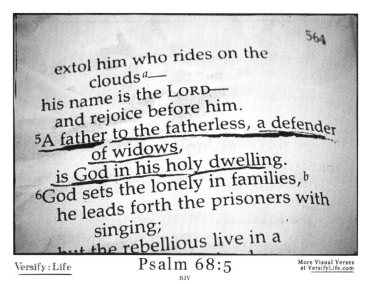

Psalm 68:5

NIV

for his son, Joseph.

After the boy lost his mother, Rebecca, Jacob's wife, Jacob makes the child a coat of many colors. Do you know why? He wanted to fill both the father and mother roles. As I read this biblical narrative, its underlying lesson became clear. Jacob was attempting to teach his son how to dance in the rain.

There's a correlation between my story and Joseph's because when I lost my father at a young age, I searched for answers but had difficulty dancing to the right tune. Yet, the Lord knew what

I was going through, and He sent His angels to teach me the art of dancing.

Every one of us is uniquely created, and from time to time, we must dance to life's varied tunes, but you are not alone. God plays an important role in each of our lives, and He is in the business of restoration. Joel 2:25 (KJV) confirms, "I will restore the years that the swarming locust has chewed."

DANCE LESSON #1:
Don't look at your life in isolation.

Although losing my dad certainly left a huge scar and could have left me isolated, an outpouring of love from my uncles turned my misery into a blessing, allowing me to grow up with an extended family in my Uncle Selvaraj's house. Everyone affectionately referred to me by my nickname, "Prabhu."

I did not have a separate room, but at night, we would roll the sheets from one end of the room to the other, and about twelve of us would share the same sheet. The beauty in it was we each knew exactly which part of the sheet was ours.

The richness of this experience cannot be expressed in words. Everything we did in that house was like a carnival, from brushing our teeth, to sharing the bathroom, to sleeping at night.

As I think back on the journey, many of the lessons learned transformed my thoughts and made a huge impact on my life, all because of the people who reached out to me. It wasn't that they knew how to dance, but like my mother, they were determined and committed to learn this art without resorting to mediocrity.

Our personal experiences and the results of our actions are constant reminders that there is much more in life to learn and appreciate. Hopefully, by the time we reach the end of this book, you will see how all the dots are well-connected in a perfect tapestry beautifully woven by the master weaver.

When Greeks die, survivors don't write a eulogy, but simply ask, "Did he or she have a passion?" How can we sustain burning passions within us when life constantly hurls at us curve balls?

In this book, I share highlights of the journey and the wonderful people who taught me how to dance. My hope and prayer are that as you partake, ultimately, pieces of my journey will help you find yours.

Finding My Faith in God

Sometimes, events that increase our wisdom also teach us how to dance. At times, it seemed every step in my life was riddled with challenges, but that thin line between hope and grace gave me all the stamina I needed to brush myself off and go forward.

At a young age, I found faith in God which is the main ingredient or substance for my hope. One's faith, I believe, is the uniting factor that keeps hope alive.

The late Evangelist Billy Graham once explained his life's road wasn't pretty, because life was filled with high and low points; therefore, we need God as our moral compass. As I am distanced from my earliest memories by time, I am

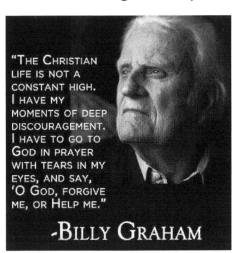

"THE CHRISTIAN LIFE IS NOT A CONSTANT HIGH. I HAVE MY MOMENTS OF DEEP DISCOURAGEMENT. I HAVE TO GO TO GOD IN PRAYER WITH TEARS IN MY EYES, AND SAY, 'O GOD, FORGIVE ME, OR HELP ME."

-BILLY GRAHAM

reminded even more of the need to appreciate, search and cherish them.

Hopefully, your search for happiness will result in your finding the true meaning for your existence. A wise man once said, "Happiness is a state of mind!"

Sometimes, God allows us to endure adversity to help us grow, learn to dance, and become better people. The lessons I learned at a young age provided me the foundation for overcoming obstacles as I walked through the valleys of dark shadows.

It's Time to Honor

The belief that heroes are merely those who help a community during natural disasters, such as a tsunami or terrorist attack, is just a myth. We often fail to recognize heroes we encounter in everyday life – those who refuse to compromise their integrity, no matter how hard the road becomes.

This book honors the amazing people who helped me rise from the streets of Chennai to San Francisco's financial district as a Senior Vice President at Bank of America. If we overlook the simple acts of kindness and genuine warmth that flows from people's hearts, we minimize their worth and begin to feel entitled. Hence, I want to give credit to all the dancers who so patiently taught me how to dance in the midst of a storm.

For this reason, I am honoring and exemplifying the characteristics of those who selflessly invested their lives in me. One of the most significant memories that I cherish most about my heroes is although none of them enjoyed significant material wealth, they all made tremendous sacrifices to share with me whatever they had.

    ☜ My uncle was one of the highest ranked officers in the city; yet, his sacrifice for me resulted in him not owning a house until he retired from work.

    ☜ He never made acquiring wealth or social status a priority. There was a thin, very disciplined line of beauty in his dance worth watching.

My list of heroes is endless, but in this book I focus specifically on those who taught me how to humbly and graciously dance, as well as on the lessons they taught me to sustain my steps even when I missed the rhythm of the beat. But first, let me introduce you to the characters who helped shaped my values:

☜ **My Uncle Selvaraj**, who has made a huge impact on my life, gave me a place to live, food to eat and sent me to school.

☜ **My mother**, a symbol of courage and determination, focused her life as a single parent on overcoming obstacles to take care of me.

✍ **Annie and Graham**, my generous sponsors,

consistently sent money from North Wales to help with my educational costs.

✍ **My Uncle John**, who was near capacity with his own responsibilities, committed to take me to the hospital every day for polio treatments, showing his agility to dance. (I was infected with the disease at an early age.)

It's mind-boggling for me to think about how generously these heroes contributed to my life for a season to exhibit their dance. Without a shadow of doubt, they exhibited their dance by paving my path to success for which I am fortunate and immensely thankful.

Therefore, each chapter ends with a thank you note.

✍ Oftentimes, we hold on to negative memories with long-lasting scars like deep etchings in a granite stone. This leads us to fret over small matters and lose our peace and happiness.

✍ If we could use precious stones to carve a painting portraying all the goodness we received along the journey, we could hold that image in our hearts forever. When the going gets tough, just remembering the kind acts heaped on us will help erase the leanness from our souls and fill our hearts with abundant joy.

As I take you through my journey, pay close attention to the ways my heroes kept the fire of hope inside me burning, so I did not get lost. Nothing worthwhile in this life comes easily, so let's make our dance steps steady and precise even when storms are raging in a torrential rainfall!

Chapter 1

A Symbol of Determination & Hope

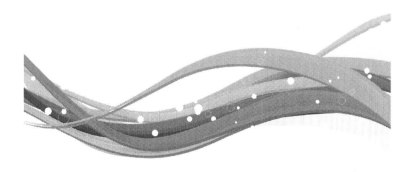

A Symbol of Determination & Hope

1

This chapter is dedicated to all the single moms who make valiant efforts to raise children in the midst of challenges.

Rarely do we recognize the sacrifices of single moms we interact with on a daily basis. Because of their unselfish love, they don't think twice about taking on multiple jobs to ensure their children are not without necessities. At the same time, they thrive to plant seeds of hope and determination through their labor, expecting them to germinate and blossom into promising futures for their children. Even when they have little or no energy, they just keep going, dancing in the rain. They, as well as anybody, realize it takes courage and effort to face the beats of life.

They give up their dreams, work multiple jobs to keep the lights on and raise their children. They work odd hours, bag groceries in stores, wait tables in restaurants and chauffeur kids around. As we come across them, we may not be able to lighten their loads, but we can make their days more enjoyable with kind words and warm smiles.

As I look back through the various segments of my life's journey, I am reminded that one of my most influential teachers was my mother who taught me how to dance in the midst of turmoil.

Although we don't get to choose our mothers, I am truly blessed to have the best, and I couldn't have asked for a better one. Her unconditional love and willpower to overcome the challenges she faced have helped me understand the difference between who I am and whose I am. As Mother Teresa once said, "The greatest gift a parent can give a child is unconditional love." That's exactly what I received from my mother. Growing up, I didn't always understand or appreciate all her sacrifices, but her simple way of life is a testament!

About my mother...

My mom grew up with only the barest necessities in Kaliyaur, a village in southern India, where there is still no electricity, indoor plumbing, water treatment system or reasonable transportation.

At a very young age, she moved with my uncle to Chennai, a densely populated metropolitan city where she had to quickly adapt to a lifestyle that was not familiar. She got married at the age of 18, but her husband abandoned her and their 6-month-old baby following a huge dispute between her and his family. In a country known for arranged marriages and a divorce rate of less than two percent, my mom had become a statistic, although not due to any fault of her own.

Unloved by her husband, she appeared to have landed on the road of hard knocks surrounded by impossibly dire circumstances; nonetheless, her hope outlived them all.

She never remarried nor looked for companionship. Instead she dedicated her life to raising me to become an honest, hard-working and distinguished man. She found her rhythm in the rain and chose a dance of serving others. I've never seen anyone quite like her who so passionately uses her heart of servanthood to spread unconditional love.

One day I asked her the motive behind her serving, and she said, "When I serve others, blessings will find their way into your life." Today, I wish I could reverse her hardships and trials, but her fortitude during hardships is what made her my hero and a wonderfully enduring dance teacher.

Dance lesson learned from my mother

It's not that she literally taught me physical dance routines, but by observing her life, I learned how to imitate her uncompromising standards. This soft-spoken, silent teacher modeled traits that, as I imitated her, would carry me through life.

DANCE LESSON 2:
When the going gets tough, the tough get going.

We've all faced unexpected and undeserved circumstances over which we've had absolutely no control. At times, they seemed to have marched toward us like an army of armored tanks as we stood by watching completely unarmed. Several times, my mother overcame situations like that. Extreme hardships sometimes pushed her to the point of committing suicide, but she found solace in her faith in God who restored her peace and calmness, so she could continue fighting.

Recently, I read a newspaper article about a woman who said she was ashamed of being poor. I thought what a contrast to my mom who was never ashamed of what she didn't have because she was so consumed with protecting me from destructive energies, especially hopelessness and self-pity.

I often wondered what caused this village girl to find such resilience and strength of character. You see, the obstacles we regret most are the ones that make us resilient. They toughen us up, so we can stand against the storms of life without being crushed.

I see a lot of similarities between my mom and a few of the widows mentioned in the Old

Testament.

After using all her resources to pay debts, the widow in 2 Kings 4:1-7 tried to prevent her creditors from taking her two sons away to work off the debts as slaves. At this point, she had been reduced to nothing. In other words, she had nothing left to live on for the rest of her life.

I am very sure that's how my mother must have felt without any resources or support from my dad. But the good news is God changed the equation, turning nothing into something.

There were times in my life when opposition tried to beat me down, but my mom's life has constantly inspired me to fight my battles without giving up. As the saying goes, when the going gets tough, the tough get going.

DANCE LESSON #3:
Don't let this world laugh at you.

When I was growing up, she would often take me to my uncle's house while she went to handle business. But as I got older, I saw her a lot less because I no longer lived with her. Whenever we were together, she always shared with me the same statement: "Don't let this world laugh at you."

Her rationale for the statement was based on the fact the world is quick to judge and laugh at you when you fall, and that's what causes you to feel humiliated. But those are the times we need to get up, move forward, view failures as mere lessons of life and treat them as stepping stones toward a brighter future.

She was saying if you stay down and defeated, you're giving the world a chance to ostracize you. In other words, she wasn't encouraging me not to fall, but to learn to quickly get back up. When I was young, I did not understand or pay attention to this truth, but as I got older, I tended to appreciate this more, especially when I found myself drifting away from the path to success.

She taught me to never give up just because circumstances were too challenging. Every one of us has to work through battles, and sometimes, the enemy we fight is invisible. Therefore, I would like to encourage you to resist the enemy and he will flee from you.

Rather than despise her plight as a single mom with very limited resources, she saw it as her calling. Her attitude inspired me to approach hurdles in my life as nothing more than a calling. With all the fortitude she had, she stopped me from wandering away from my destiny and forced me to refocus, so that I could differentiate between the good life and a mediocre one.

One of her primary missions in life was to see me grow up and become a respectable human being. She was a praying woman whose faith in God was unshakable.

DANCE LESSON #4:
Give what I have in my hand.

All she had at her disposal was her faith. She didn't have an education, skills, property or money. Most of her life, she lived with different family members, taking care of the sick and elderly and preparing the meals.

My mother is a gentle, small-framed woman with a huge heart, a heart so large it readily welcomes and accommodates anyone who needs help.

Most of her life, she has lived with family members and has taken care of the sick and elderly. Whether spending long hours in a hospital or preparing food for several people, my mom does it eagerly and without complaining as if she were serving her own family.

The quality of her character has truly been an asset to many, but what amazes me is how her virtue seemed to have manifested on its own. It makes her welcomed among people she meets from all walks of life and fills her friends and family with joy.

Regardless of how grand our visions are, until God can trust us with what little we have in our hands, how can He trust us with more?

DANCE LESSON #5:
Never Compromise on your Prayer life!

Even though my mother had to overcome many personal trials, her faith in God was unshakable. She would never compromise about going to church or placing problems in the hand of God.

"There is no power like that of prevailing prayer - of Abraham pleading for Sodom, Jacob wrestling in the stillness of the night, Moses standing in the breach, Hannah intoxicated with sorrow, David heartbroken with remorse and grief, Jesus in sweat and blood. Add to this list from the records of the church your personal observation and experience, and always there is cost of passion unto blood. Such prayer prevails."

Samuel Chadwick, renowned British minister and author known, during the turn of the century, for his teachings on spirit-filled prayer.

I could add to this list from my personal observations and experiences with my mother. There was always a cost to the passion she had, and her prayers were the source of her strength.

Prayer turns ordinary mortals into people of power; it brings God to the rescue.

I strongly believe that her trust in the Lord and her prayers were instrumental in protecting me from falling apart. Also, there was a consistency in her prayer life, possibly because she saw it as the only rope at her disposal.

Even though we don't always agree on everything, I respect her greatly for what she has done for me.

If you are a single mom who feels the perils of life are sucking the breath out of you, depleting your strength and stifling your will to take another step forward, don't give up! This book has been written especially for you.

I'm convinced that if God can send angels and resources to give strength and courage to my mother, He will do the same for you. It won't be long before your silent tears are turned to joy. So, do not give up on your sons and daughters, but consistently show them love, regardless of the circumstances.

There's not a shadow of doubt in my mind that you will find the hope and determination to keep moving forward in the midst of the valley. Even though I'm ending this chapter with a thank you note, it's also a love letter to my mother.

To my mother:
Thanks for pouring your life into my life and for all the priceless lessons I have learned from you.

✍ Thank you for being there and for your countless sacrifices.

✍ How could I have made it without your heart-felt prayers? Your prayers have always uplifted me. and clung to me all my life. They surface as a thin line of grace even when I can't immediately see the results with my naked eyes.

Whether I face overwhelmingly hectic days or uneventful days of routine tasks, the lessons I learned from your dancing will continue to guide me.

Are You Dancing in the Rain?

Thursday
July 10, 2008

THE MATTHEWS
RECORD

YOUR LOCAL NEWSPAPER

Vol 3   Issue 6

Above: Celebrating their first 4th of July since coming to America from India, Chinnammal and Celine, (last names are not used in India) are all smiles and full of pride as they participate in the Peoples' Parade in downtown matthews Last Friday. Below: A very patriotically dressed Brennan Cash, the Matthews Parks And Rec. summer intern, was busy handing out American Flags.

MATTHEWS 4TH OF JULY CELEBRATION

Independence Forever

This past Fourth of July marked the 225th anniversary of the Declaration of Independence and to what Thomas Jefferson called "the declaratory charter of our rights."

The true significance of the Declaration is not to any conventional law or political contract but to the equal rights possessed by all men. It is in this sense that Abraham Lincoln praised "the man who, in the concrete pressure of a struggle for national independence by a single people, had the coolness, forecast, and capacity to introduce into a merely revolutionary document, an abstract truth, applicable to all men and all times."

When John Adams was asked to prepare a statement on the 50th anniversary of the Declaration of Independence, he delivered just two words: "Independence Forever."

Did you know?

Fifty six individuals from each of the original 13 colonies participated in the Second Continental Congress and signed the Declaration of Independence.

Nine of the signers were immigrants, two were brothers, two were cousins, and one was an orphan. The average age of a signer was 45. The oldest delegate was Benjamin Franklin, who was 70. The youngest was Edward Lynch Jr. of South Carolina, who was 27. Eighteen of the signers were merchants or businessmen, fourteen were farmers, four were doctors, and twenty two were lawyers. Seventeen of the signers served in the military during the American Revolution. Five of the signers were captured by the British during the war and eleven had their homes and property destroyed.

MORE INSIDE: PHOTOS OF OUR CELEBRATION, PAGE 12

(Top right to left: My mother, Celine, and Aunt Chinnammal)
wave American flags at Independence Day parade.

ENDNOTES
Reference:
Author: Samuel Chadwick, Book: The Path of Prayer

Chapter 2

A Man of Integrity

A Man of Integrity

2

This chapter is dedicated to all mentors who serve as father figures by guiding and shaping the lives of children through sacrificial acts of kindness.

As I've thought deeply about exactly how I was able to continue my journey toward my destination, I realized the mentors who crossed my path were a common element influencing each twist and turn. While there is no doubt that I've done my portion of the work, taken the risks and pushed myself to the edge, it would be arrogant to say that I've done it all using my own strength. I've been influenced by many great people who have had and continue to have a notable impact on my thought processes and decision-making.

My Mentor and Father Figure

Uncle Selvaraj, my mother's brother, is my father figure and the dominant influence in my life. To simply say he is my role model would be an understatement, since I owe everything that I have to him. But we will traverse through his life as I highlight the dance lessons I learned from him.

In life we have to make choices every day. Right or wrong is defined by the principles and values we believe and uphold; yet, each decision has consequences.

The person who prevails is the one who makes higher moral choices when their principles are put to the ultimate test. We come across so many people in our lives, but some leave positive legacies and lasting impacts as substance to pattern our lives by.

✍ Uncle Selvaraj was one such father figure, and I am privileged to have him as mine.

When I look at his life, like a treasure, it always prompts me to search for answers to questions like: Is there a moment in life that defines a person? Or is it the vastness of talent and years of experience they possess that separate them from others? Let's take a closer look at his life to find the lessons we can learn from his dance.

There is no substitute for perseverance and hard work.

My uncle grew up with seven brothers and sisters in a very small village without electricity and at times lacked other basic necessities. He always knew that to improve his living conditions, he had to study harder, get a college degree, then move to a city and find a job.

To achieve this goal, he had to walk several miles daily to school, and in order to study, since there was no electricity, he had to find a place to sit near a window, or find somewhere with a bright light.

He studied with vigor and determination, and in

the early 1950s, he finished his Bachelor of Economics Degree and found a stable job.

With all its perplexities, life can be hard to comprehend. Your life experiences may differ greatly from mine and my uncle's, so, this is not an attempt to undermine or belittle your situation. But if we focus our attention on working harder and consistently making the right choices, the purpose for our lives will overpower our deficiencies.

Nothing in this world can take the place of hard work and persistence, both of which my uncle has pushed to the fullest.

DANCE LESSON #6:
Do not compromise when your integrity is tested.

A study conducted determined the most important attribute for successful people is integrity. One dangerous stumbling block for persons of integrity is to compromise their standards when faced with tough choices. My Uncle Selvaraj lived one of the most honorable and exemplary lives I had ever seen.

Even when he would have clearly benefited financially, he refused to compromise his integrity. His example demonstrates the height of his character, as well as the honorable legacy he left behind for his children:

One time as Uncle Selvaraj worked as a high-ranking city official, a $7 Million dollar unaccounted for fund (easily worth 15 times more today) sat in the city's treasury, but it was never documented in the government ledger. That meant he was one of only a few people who knew the fund existed. One day, his supervisor approached him asking, "Given the nature of this fund, why don't we split this money among ourselves?"

Although it was a lucrative offer, Uncle Sel was not blinded by greed or want. Instead he warned his manager to return the money to the government immediately or else he would report it as stolen to the appropriate authorities. Faced with no choice, his supervisor put the money back into the government treasury.

What's ironic is my uncle didn't even own a house or a piece of land on which to build a house. He was living in a rental house; yet, he stood on the principles of his conviction which caused him to maintain a higher standard of life.

He declined many opportunities to get rich through shortcuts, such as this, but chose not to compromise his standards which allowed him to sleep peacefully at night. It wasn't until after he retired that he bought his first home using his pension fund.

It takes a sacrifice to leave a legacy behind. Owning a home or improving the quality of life for his immediate family was not his highest priority. Over the years, Uncle Selvaraj cultivated the same values in his wife and children which explains why the light he left behind shines as a legacy for many. Don't compromise, even when it costs you!

DANCE LESSON #7:
Treat everyone with love and respect.

One thing that amazes me about his life is how he treated everyone with special care through simple gestures, like remembering people's special occasions. He was very prompt in sending birthday cards, calling on wedding anniversaries or just being there in time of need for moral support. He always carried a phone book in his hand (talk about the PDA of the 60's) to call and wish relatives and associates well.

He genuinely cared for others and went all out to show kindness. The incident I'm about to describe shows one key attribute that separated him from everyone else in my life.

✍ When I went to college, he was a chief officer in Pudukottai, a nearby town in southern India.

On my first day at college, I was standing in a long line to pay my fees. Trust me, when I say a long line, it was really a humongous line with just two counters open to serve all departments. My uncle had already given me the money to pay my fees, but unexpectedly, he showed up!

✍ He had taken a day off from work to come and stand in the line with me! All I could think of was he must have realized that when all the other kids were standing in line with their parents, I would be standing alone.

✍ At this point he is a government official; yet, he traveled three to four hours from his office on public transportation to stand in line with me. He could have easily called someone from the town where I was studying and had them take care of this matter for him. But he wanted to handle it personally and be there to give attention to the details.

✍ He wanted to make sure I was properly placed in college, so he played the role of my father.

✍ He always put himself in others' shoes to identify with what they were going through. He

*My uncle Selvaraj,
Man of Integrity,
works at his desk.*

was a true representation of the Bible verse in Mark 12:31 (NLT), which says, "Love your neighbor as yourself."

✍ In that same way, when I got my first job, he showed up in the town where I worked and stayed with me for the first week to make sure I was living comfortably in my new place.

✍ He gave fatherly advice on how I should live and spoke with my colleagues at work. He wished me well and then returned to his workplace.

DANCE LESSON #8:
Tailor your life to serve others.

It is a rare quality for anyone to tailor his life to concentrate on the welfare of others, but Uncle Sel did. I thought my uncle took such extra care of me because he loved me more than anyone else, but when I saw what he did for my other cousins and nephews, I realized he did the same things for everyone as they were growing up and paid just as much attention to their minute details as he did to mine.

Uncle Selvaraj and Aunt Chinnammal celebrate their 25th wedding anniversary.

✍ When I went to India recently on personal business, I visited some of my nephews who had gotten married after I moved to the states. As I browsed through their family pictures and wedding albums, I found out how integrally my uncle was involved in their lives, especially around their wedding activities.

✍ The love and respect we have for him is mutual, and that may be why close family and friends honored him by asking him to play a key role during important milestones in their lives.

✍ As the eldest son, he carried a lot of family-related responsibilities by himself. So after he moved to the city, he slowly moved his family there, one by one, and helped them get settled, find jobs and get married.

When I think of my uncle, I'm reminded of this famous quote from Andrew Carnegie: "As I grow older, I pay less attention to what men say. I just watch what they do."

DANCE LESSON #9:
Live a simple life in order to leave a legacy.

As pastor and author, William Arthur Ward, once said, *"Each of us will one day be judged by our standard of life – not by our standard of living; by our measure of giving – not by our measure of wealth; by our simple goodness – not by our seeming greatness."*

I will always remember Uncle Selvaraj as an honorable man with a simple life and a role model whose legacy is a benchmark for others.

✍ Through many more small encounters with him, he made significant impacts on my life. For instance, when he was a high-ranking deputy collector in a nearby city, I had the privilege of staying with him for a couple of days in his government apartment. I was amazed at how content he was staying in a one-bedroom apartment.

✍ He had a handful of garments, which could all fit in one suitcase and only one pair of shoes. At the end of each day, he wrote down every expense in a notebook.

✍ If we analyze his lifestyle, when it comes to what he possessed, he never acted as owner of anything but as a steward who refused to squander the resources entrusted to him by God.

As you can tell, his lifestyle had a huge influence on me, so I'm turning this message into a thank you note. If I could dance half as well as he did, I would consider my life complete.

To Uncle Selvaraj:

I say, thank you for all your investments in my life. Thank you for teaching me to be accountable for my actions, as well as for my words.

I seek to model my life after such a simple and exemplary manner. A lot of times, we search for the right words to advise others, but actions speak louder than words, and you were a great example of that principle.

✍ Thank you for teaching me your value system: Character is more valuable than appearance. Relationships mean more than money. People mean more than things. When we begin to assume this value system, it becomes evident that we are maturing.

✍ Thank you for teaching me to value meaningful relationships. When my life gets busy, I may unknowingly overlook another's needs. Your life has shown me that I should carve out time to invest in meaningful relationships like you did.

✍ Like a boomerang effect, the power of your virtues not only impact my life, but the lives of others I am touching in return.

ENDNOTES
Quotes used from :
Andrew Carnegie (Scottish born American Industrialist and Philanthropist. 1835-1919)
William Arthur Ward quotes (American dedicated scholar, author, editor, pastor and teacher)

Chapter 3

A Woman with an Abundance Mindset

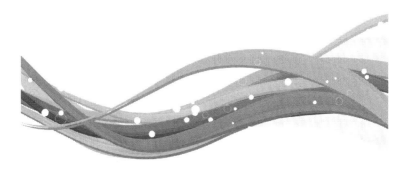

A Woman with an Abundance Mindset

3

This chapter is dedicated to action takers who act when they see a need.

"A bruised reed He will not break, and smoking flax He will not quench (Isaiah 42:3)." The Prophet Isaiah uses the phrase "bruised reed" to describe something that is fragile and weak.

> ✍ It symbolizes people who have been broken or who are about to be broken. When people are hurt and wounded, feeble and weak, they lose their sense of self-worth.

Not wanting to waste time on them, the world is quick to write them off as weak and hopeless. The right response would be finding ways to serve one another in the spirit of compassion and humility. The human race survives due to the existence of good-hearted people.

A woman who showed genuine care

My Aunt Chinnammal is genuinely concerned about and interested in the wellbeing of others which is commonly expressed in her actions. She was the answer to my mother's prayer for a miracle, and it transformed my life.

Few people really have an abundance mentality. My aunt is one who possesses such a rare characteristic. I have never seen her do anything out of selfish motives. She has always seemed consumed with making sure others were taken care of. Instead of demanding the comfortable lifestyle she deserved and could afford, she made countless sacrifices to share with her husband the responsibilities of providing shelter to many family members.

She was heaven-sent to my mother who sought every possible way to manage the household expenses, so she could raise me.

✍ My mother and I were living in a small two-room house with a kitchen and a bedroom. When she came to the end of her rope, trying to feed her son and keep a roof over our heads, she must have cried out to God like Hagar, Sarah's handmaid.

✍ I am very certain my mother was looking for a miracle every day. Oftentimes, we expect miracles to be delivered by angels with wings, but hers didn't arrive with a dramatic entrance but through ordinary events.

The biggest miracles come to us in small packages.

One evening when my Aunt Chinnammal came to visit my mother and me, she brought some cookies. It is a common custom in India not to visit anyone empty-handed, so guests typically bring fruit, biscuits, flowers or sweets.

✍ As my aunt was talking to my mother, she opened the cookie pack for me. A few minutes later when she turned around to look for me, to her surprise, I had finished the entire pack of cookies, as if I haven't eaten in days.

✍ As she left our house a little later, she couldn't stop thinking about how quickly I had consumed the cookies. Her heart was so troubled, she knew she had to do something; so, she sent Uncle John, my mother's younger brother, to bring me to her house to live.

Her compassionate act was the rope the Lord provided me as a way to hang on. At some point in everyone's life, God gives hope in the form of a rope like that. Sometimes, we ignore a little help expecting dramatic changes.

Our attitudes during our sufferings and our ability to endure are testimonies God uses to reach other people. Going to live with my aunt may sound like a small turn of events, but ultimately it changed the trajectory of my life.

✍ I am sure my mother would have done everything possible to raise me, but at the same time, I don't want to minimize the generosity of my uncle and aunt who raised me as their own child. The sense of family and stability there provided the foundation on which I still stand.

✍ Aunt Chinnammal's house has been a shelter for many people over the years, not just for me.

We must believe that things happen for a reason, and when we are given a blessing, we should grab it with both hands.

On the other hand, if you get a chance to help someone, don't wait for everything to fall in place. We don't know what may happen to the person sitting next to you on an airplane or standing behind you in the grocery store line. The chance my aunt gave me opened the floodgates of opportunity to stabilize my life.

DANCE LESSON #10:
It is easy to get bad name, but hard to sustain the good name.

Every time my aunt got a chance to feed me, she not only gave me food for my physical body, but she shared words of wisdom for my mental strength. One thing she always wanted me to remember was, "It is easy to get bad name, but hard to sustain the good name."

In other words, "You have to work really hard to do good things consistently to be considered a good person." That may be one way we can differentiate between a good life and a mediocre one.

DANCE LESSON #11:
Don't complain!

Left to right: Aunt Chinnammal,
my mother, Celine, & my wife, Jay

After I moved to the United States, my aunt was able to spend about six months with us. During that time, I noticed another admirable quality in her, which was her ability to appreciate everything and never complain about anything.

If only the children of Israel had learned that lesson sooner, they may have entered the promised land and alleviated years of wandering in the wilderness. The uncomplaining spirit comes from a position of power. Complaining is the fruit of a thankless heart, and it rarely aligns with God's perspective. Losing patience is a sign of weakness. My Aunt Chinnammal was not always like this, but somehow life has taught her these beautiful lessons. I cherish the qualities and pray that someday, I will be able to understand how she learned to dance to this tune.

We shared a love that is beyond what I can explain in this chapter, but I want to send this token of my love, as a thank you note to her:

✍ It's easy to say a simple "Thanks," but it is going to take a lifetime to live by what you have taught me.

✍ I greatly appreciate you, Aunt Chinnammal, not just for bringing me into your home, but for the many contributions you have made throughout my life.

My aunt and mother visit an amusement park bordering North and South Carolina.

Chapter 4

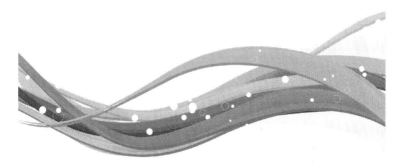

A Woman of Commitment

Are You Dancing in the Rain?

A Woman of Commitment

4

This chapter is dedicated to social
workers who spend countless hours
helping people in need, especially the
selfless human beings who serve the less
fortunate in foreign lands.

Growth can be sustained only when we serve consistently.

We all have a desire to do good for others; that's an inborn quality. When we watch movies, we identify ourselves with the heroes who rescue people from trouble. Even when it comes to real life, we tend to agree with the sentiment of Winston Churchill, who once said, "I never worry about action, but only inaction."

I met someone early in my life who was energized by doing good for others. Her name is Sarojini Fernando.

> ✍ *She was the recipient of several awards, including a national award for social work from the President of India.*

> ✍ She rendered services to underprivileged children and battered women.

> ✍ She was an ambassador of commitment and service.

When I was young, I had the privilege of meeting her for a brief moment at a family event. During that time, she was very polite and warm. When I think about that conversation now, I remember how she did not waste time with meaningless talk but was interested in knowing every last detail about my life. That one interaction laid a foundation through which she became a huge contributor to my education.

Unless God says it is done, it is not done. Sarojini was able to put the interest of others in front of her own. There are some people who actually listen and think at the same time, and I am very sure Sarojini has that ability.

Soon after I met her, she made arrangements to take care of my educational necessities like tuition, fees, school uniforms and books. She also introduced me to a local organization called the Guild of Service that supports kids in third world countries through the generosity of people from developed western countries.

Through connections I made with Sarojini and the Guild of Service, I had the privilege of meeting two other people I would like to introduce. Annie and Graham are the two angels I came across who assisted me from a distance.

✍ For over 10 years, they regularly sent money to pay for my school fees, books and uniforms.

✍ Except in photos, we have never seen each other and probably never will during this lifetime because they live in North Wales, Australia.

✍ In the beginning, I wrote letters to them in broken English, but they never focused on my mistakes. Instead, they continued to send grace-filled letters that encouraged me to not give up on my education.

If you are going through a rough time, or if you feel like you are in the middle of the valley and worried about the uncertainty of this life, the one thing I can tell you is **please don't give up or lose heart**. Our responsibility is to continue the good fight and use our resources wisely; then, the fruit of our labor will lead us to a good life.

✍ Just like a wise man once said, "Don't let our past dictate who we are, but let it be a part of who we will become." Unless my God says it is done, the work is still undone.

The events in my life were beautifully orchestrated and networked by God. Annie and Graham came into my life for a season and poured out the goodness I needed for that moment, and they did not expect anything in return.

We can become passive contributors in others' lives, which is not wrong, but it takes time and energy to become active contributors like Annie and

Graham. They took time to find out how I was doing and encouraged me to believe in who I was by constantly writing letters to me and meeting my monetary needs.

As 19th Century British Prime Minister Benjamin Disraeli once said, "A consistent soul believes in destiny."

> ✍ A few years later, Sarojini gave me my first job. Right after I finished college, she trusted me with the opportunity to work for one year under her leadership in a project hosted by the Danish Embassy.

> ✍ During that time, we had a chance to spend precious moments together, whether traveling to remote villages near the southern part of India, or talking over lunch. We talked about numerous topics from politics to social events and family, but never once did she speak negatively or critically of anyone.

Matthew 15:11 (NASB) says, *"It is not what enters into the mouth that defiles the man, but what proceeds out of the mouth, that defiles the man."*

DANCE LESSON #12:
Remember the small conversations.

Sometimes, we spend hours engaging in conversations with strangers we meet on trains, buses or planes, but the majority of those relationships end as soon as we walk away from them. A lot of times, we make empty promises which we never intend to follow through to completion.

✍ **Love others as yourself.** This is the "Golden Rule." Where there is love, there is a lot of patience and the ability to see others' needs as your own. That's what I saw in Sarojini's eyes. She didn't do that just for me, but for many others she came across.

✍ There's a difference between interest and commitment. When you're interested in doing something, you do it only when circumstances permit. When you're committed to something, you accept no excuses, only results. It was commitment I saw in people like Sarojini, Annie and Graham. These are angels who never even took a small conversation lightly, but instead genuinely cared for others.

What amazed me the most about Sarojini is the depth of her dedication and how she worked long hours for the cause that she believed in. She always acknowledged the good things that I was doing and appreciated me, which has been a constant source of encouragement. She never married but always enjoyed her extended family.

Another thing I learned from her is that treasures are not only found at the end of the journey but all along the way.

Sarojini never took credit for the contributions she made in my life. She always stood by the sideline and enjoyed seeing me grow.

After I passed through the stage of dependency and moved to the United States, I had a chance to see her once during my visit back home. I saw the gentle pride in her smile. That's probably the only gift that I gave back to her for all the blessings she showered on me.

One of the key ingredients to being successful or achieving greater goals in life is to do the right things <u>consistently</u>.

To Sarojini:

✍ Thank you, Sarojini, for showing me your kindness and goodness. You have left behind a vacancy that is hard to fill.

✍ Thank you for teaching me how to make a difference in others' lives.

✍ Even though you are not with us now, may your soul rest in peace.

Chapter 5

Quitting is Not an Option

Quitting is Not an Option

This chapter is dedicated to brothers
and sisters who are infected with polio,
but strive to make a difference in spite
of their obstacles.

As human beings, our natural instinct is to get out of trouble by running away from it. We tend to give up on dreams without persevering in our efforts to reach our destiny.

As my pastor used to say, "When the going gets tough, the tough get going." This applies even when we find ourselves in dire circumstances or at rock bottom. We must find ways to hold on to any ray of hope that will lead us to higher ground.

When I was about six months old, I suffered from a high fever.

> ✍ *The fever was caused by a virus, which led to Polio, a disease that paralyzes one's nervous system and damages or destroys the nerves that send messages from the brain to the muscles.*

> ✍ *The truth is, this is one of the best things that has happened in my life. I might have lost the functioning of key nerves in my legs, but without this setback, I would not have experienced the heroic deeds of many and their commitment to help put this life of mine together.*

I would like to introduce my Uncle John. There are several dance lessons I learned from him, and here are some of the golden nuggets:

Learn the art of survival.

The highlight of what Uncle John imparted to me is the survival mechanism.

He had to overcome many hurdles in his personal life, but I have never seen him dwell in the past. Some people would lose their sanity if they didn't have basic resources like money to take care of the bare necessities.

During the festivals in India, there is a tradition of buying new clothes for everyone in the family. As I mentioned earlier, ours is a large family; so, to take care of everyone at the time of festivities is a huge task.

- ✍ Although Uncle John did not have much money, he made sure we had enough food and basic necessities at home.

- ✍ He knew the value of family and made it his highest priority. The biggest lesson that I learned from him is how to survive and take care of the family, even when nothing seems to go the right way.

Learn to negotiate and come up with a win/win solution.

I have never seen Uncle John walk out of a room with a win-some, lose-some attitude.

✍ During my school days, I did not pay much attention to studies and constantly got into trouble. At one important juncture of my academic life, which was 10th grade, I failed miserably. Tenth grade was the most critical school year because that's when students in India selected their college majors.

✍ For most people, failing academically means their life is pretty much over from an

QUITTING IS NOT AN OPTION

educational perspective. I was shocked by my own failure and was looking desperately to rewind the course of my school year. Uncle John knew what I was going through. He knew

I could have done better and believed I should be given a second chance to prove myself.

He knew education was a foundation for life, and if I did not finish school, my opportunity for succeeding in life would have been very difficult.

✍ He took me to school and convinced the principal to give me a second chance, and to my utter surprise, I was re-admitted to the school.

✍ I am sure Uncle John used everything he had at his disposal to get me back in school. He would never have walked out of that room until he had convinced the principal of why I needed a second chance.

Have you ever fought desperately for something as if you had no other options? That's exactly what my uncle did for me that day.

✍ Because of his valiant effort, I was not only able to finish 10th grade at that school, but I also moved on to the 11th grade there without any additional hurdles.

✍ Science is the subject that I failed in the 10th grade, but I took science as my major for the next two years of high school. What Uncle

John taught me that day was to never quit, even when you are down and out. His confidence in me caused me to become extremely competitive when it came to my school work. As a result, I finished in the top percentile in science.

✍ Later, I studied computer science at that same school, and those courses paved a way for me to come to the United States and work in some prestigious organizations.

Talk about rewriting the chapters of one's life...

We all constantly make choices in life. Some help us write our stories better, but each story can be rewritten several times over the course of our journey.

✍ They can be rewritten when angels come along and reroute the direction for our lives. They come for a season and invest selflessly. To write a better story of your life, take a moment to seriously conduct inventory of all the people in it.

Proverbs 28:26 says, *"Those who walk in wisdom are kept safe."* Ask for God's wisdom, so you can be kept safe from disasters.

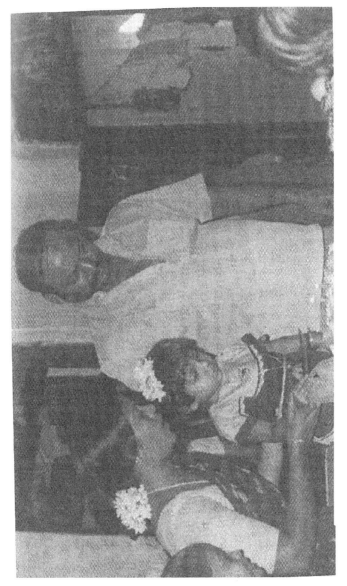

Uncle John celebrates a birthday with his daughter.

Unconditional love is without expectations.

This characteristic is something that I found common in both Uncle John and my mother. As Benjamin Franklin once said, "Well done is better than well said." During my initial stages of polio, my right leg was twisted in the opposite direction.

Someone had to take me to the hospital every day, wait in line for my turn to go through physiotherapy and then drop me off at school. Uncle John and my mother did this for the first five years.

✐ Every day, they had to hang a sandbag to straighten and twist the leg back to its normal position, and this procedure had to be repeated at home, as well. Under any circumstance, this was a huge undertaking.

✍ As a result, today, I am able to walk normally like any other person.

These types of selfless acts also require patience, unconditional love and determination.

This experience has given me a great deal of respect for people who are physically challenged; yet, continue their day-to-day lives without disruption.

Common dance lessons we learn from people who never quit:

✍ They are not looking for sympathy, but they are aggressively looking for ways to prove themselves.

Creative Thinkers
So many of the world's great achievers like Walt Disney, who suffered from dyslexia; Abraham Lincoln and Winston Churchill, both of whom had physical challenges, inspired people to stay hopeful and continue pressing forward.

When an 18-month-old baby does not show any signs of speech, the parents become anxious and worried.

✎ The fact is children develop physical gestures to creatively express what they want in the absence of speech, and that helps them to become creative thinkers in the long term.

✎ The same is true of people who are physically challenged; they have to be creative in using other resources to compensate for the absence of a functioning body part.

When I look back at the health obstacles I faced as a child, I am reminded that it wasn't an easy journey. Things looked bleak at times, but they taught me to be patient and not give up hope by looking at events in isolation.

To my Uncle John:

✎ Thank you for being there and showing me unconditional love.

✎ Thank you for teaching me not to quit, even in the midst of adversity.

This quote by Oscar Wilde, an Irish playwright and poet, appropriately summarizes Uncle John. "We are all in the gutter, but some of us are looking at the stars." It was Uncle John who taught me how to look at the stars.

Chapter 6

God Is Just A Prayer Away

Are You Dancing in the Rain?

God Is Just A Prayer Away

6

This chapter is dedicated to fathers who
are role models for their children.

When we go through times of trouble, we sometimes ask the age-old question, "Where is God in all this?" or "Is my faith real?"

When we feel numb from all the hurts and pains that drive us to serious pondering, we need to find a moment to quiet our minds and be still, knowing that God is just a prayer away.

✎ Mother Teresa once said, "I know God will not give me anything I can't handle. I just wish that He didn't trust me so much."

✎ No one on earth is perfectly safe and immune from adversities, but all of us may need to pray like Mother Teresa that they should not hit us so hard.

✎ It's very easy to place enormous faith in the Lord when everything is going great, but when adversity comes knocking on our doors, many of us will start to lose our faith in God.

Sometimes, God allows certain things to happen for reasons which we as humans have a hard time understanding. Below I share with you an incident that taught me how to dance when things were completely out of control.

My daughter, a walking miracle

In this chapter, I am going to talk about my daughter, Sruthi. I have never expressed in words how much I love her. She is the most beautiful young girl that I have ever met.

> ✍ She has a very strong personality and has gone through quite a few trials at a young age. I am not sure if she acquired her strong mental traits from me, or if she has just always possessed them, but I have always been amazed by them.

The incident I am about to share with you occurred during the early days of our family. Sruthi was two and half years old, still very energetic and full of inquisitive childhood innocence.

To give you a picture of how analytical her thought patterns were, when the main character in the "Bob the Builder" TV show she was watching searched for a hammer to pound in a nail, she grabbed a hammer and ran toward the TV to help straighten the nail.

It seemed like an ordinary day until I got a call at work from my wife with panic in her voice. She told me to come to the children's hospital in Oakland not far from our house. My daughter, who had always been active, was not able to get out of bed. Although she had been sick for a week, we assumed she had a fever and a cold, so we were not greatly concerned. While I worked, my wife spent her days at the hospital with her, but the doctors were not able to diagnose her condition.

    ✍ Since her condition was not improving, a pediatrician recommended we take her to another children's hospital for more tests.

    ✍ After the initial tests and X-rays, a specialist told my wife the illness looked serious but did not say what he thought it was, so I rushed to the hospital to find out what was going on.

I could feel anxiety building in the room as the specialists and doctors discussed their expert opinions.

After a couple of hours of discussion, the doctors told us our daughter had emphysema and that the phlegm in her lungs had spilled and covered her entire chest. Ordinarily, they said she would have been thought to be too young to acquire this disease, but unfortunately, she had been hit with it.

Due to hospital rules, only one parent was

permitted to stay after 9 p.m., so they asked that one of us leave. I asked my wife to go home and get some rest, so I could stay.

As the night progressed, doctors continued working on her, but she got worst. Around midnight, they told me she urgently needed surgery.

As part of normal procedure, the administrative staff handed me several documents to sign before they could take her in for surgery.

All I could think about up to that point was how cute, active and full of energy my daughter was. But suddenly I was forced to see her in another dimension, which was a bit unsettling and unfamiliar to me. But only the strength that God can give upheld me and assured me Sruthi's surgery was in His hands.

Several doctors were running tests, and at one point, she refused to take the oxygen mask. As I held her hand, I told her, "Don't worry, honey. Everything is going to be alright. Let them help us get through this." Even though she was exhausted, by this point, she revealed her inner strength; she didn't want to cry out loud, but tears rolled down her cheeks. It certainly was not the level of maturity I had expected to see in a two-and-a-half-year-old toddler.

✎ A gust of fear weighed heavily on my heart. I didn't want to inform my wife that night and cause her more fear, so I reached out to my pastor, Ranjan Samuel, and asked the church to pray for her, since I knew they were meeting that night to prepare for a Good Friday service.

The doctors estimated the surgery would take two or three hours, and she was taken into the operating room around midnight.

✎ By this time, I was practically in a zombie state since I had been there and awake for more than 17 hours.

As Henri Nouwen, a Dutch Catholic priest and author, once said, "Prayer is a radical conversion of all our mental processes because in prayer we move away from ourselves, our worries, preoccupation, and self-gratification— and direct all that we recognize as ours to God in the simple trust that through His love all will be made new."

✎ I had no strength left to pray long prayers, but I told God I wanted to go home with my daughter alive. This prayer came to my mind several times throughout the night.

As time seemed to creep by, I watched for the operating room theatre doors to open, but they didn't. The clock on the wall ticked from three to four, from five to six with every single minute starting to advance slower and slower.

After six and a half hours, they brought her out of surgery into a special care unit.

✍ The doctors explained to me why the surgery had taken so long. They had to move slowly to avoid the risk of puncturing her lungs as they scraped phlegm from them. But something really peculiar happened when they placed the lungs back into her chest. They immediately filled with air all by themselves and ballooned up perfectly like healthy lungs.

The doctor said he didn't know where the air had come from, or how it had filled her lungs. Even though it took the doctors by surprise, I know it was a miracle. God was gracious to hear my prayers and answer them at the right moment.

✍ Sruthi's next 15 days of recovery in the hospital were filled with several miracles. It made me realize just how close our God is when we are going through trials and tribulations and what a privilege we have to reach out to Him in prayer.

My daughter fully recovered and left the hospital. Until this day, I only see her as a walking miracle. God has been good to our family, and we are absolutely grateful for that. Not all serious trials have happy endings, but if you are going through a tough time, the next few paragraphs were written to help strengthen your belief and conviction.

Cyril Prabhu and daughter, Sruthi

Here is the dance I learned from this incident:

✍ No matter what happens to us, God is in control. He will never leave us nor forsake us. It is not the trials or hardships triggered by them that cause lasting damage, but how we respond in the midst of the fire. It may be hard to remain still and calm, but that's when we must ask God for strength. Just like in the case of my daughter, the Lord will give you the strength and courage to get through it.

✍ The Bible tells us that we are saved by grace through **faith.**

✍ Our faith and belief levels are our lifelines to the Lord. Our personal relationships with God are only as good as our faith and trust in Him. The stronger your faith is in the Lord, the deeper your personal relationship will become with Him.

✍ Family and friends are great assets when we go through trials that are out of our control.

✍ When we were going through hard times, there were so many people not related to me who were offering prayers from everywhere.

✍ People would come to the hospital and bring food for every meal. They would stop by and comfort us with kind words.

✍ We were always surrounded by beautiful people who were willing to go the extra mile to care for the wellbeing of others.
By the same token, I don't want to belittle the problems that you face. The hardships that you are up against could possibly be even more extreme.

You may even feel like you are literally going through a fiery furnace due to the heat and intensity.

What I can assure you of based on this experience is that every hope that we can cling to can only come from God.

    ✎ Don't give up on your faith. Even when you think you don't have energy to stand up and face the trials, be strong and courageous.

    ✎ One thing I am absolutely certain about, without a shadow of doubt, is when we reach out to God in our helpless situations, He will reveal His strength.

Remember, God is only a prayer away!

ENDNOTES
    Author: Henri **Nouwen**, *Book:* <u>*Wounded Prophet; A Portrait of Henri J.M.*</u> **Nouwen**

Chapter 7

Hardships Happen!
But Don't Ever Lose Hope!

Are You Dancing in the Rain?

Hardships Happen!
But Don't Ever Lose Hope!

7

This chapter is dedicated to my family who has stood by my side, giving me comfort and motivation every day to look toward the future with a smile.

I am absolutely convinced that the resources we strive to possess can never help us move forward in life, but it is our attitude about life that determines our destiny and is far more essential than the opportunities, money, circumstances or even failures.

    ✍ I have listened to many debates about how we don't have control over our fate or destiny.

    ✍ The compelling testimony below confirms that we do have control over our decisions and actions.

Good intentions are not enough; you need a solid plan and an exit strategy.

After being in the states for several years, I wanted to use my talents and resources to do something to help my community by creating new jobs, especially for young graduates just coming out of college without any experience. I believed this new venture would serve as a platform to help them prove themselves.

    ✍ I started a new company in India to provide end-to-end construction as a supplier to the hospitality industry. In order to build a quality product, I hired highly skilled architects to manage the day-to-day operations and execution of the project.

✍ The company was established to help young people succeed, and that was basically the premise behind my well-intentioned expectations.

✍ Since I was managing the team from the US, I had to make several trips to India every year to keep the team encouraged. I also worked long hours at night managing the company and adjusting cost and production strategies to keep the business going.

✍ After four long years of hard work and determination, the product was completed, and we were starting to distribute it to major hotels and restaurants in southern India.

Starting a business is a great idea, especially if you have a product that is marketable. But things did not turn out the way I expected. One problem led to another, and arriving at work one morning, I learned I needed to shut down the business with a huge loss -- indebtedness of over $250,000 in loans and lines of credit.

Sometimes problems show up in bunches, rather than individually. To make matters worse, one of my employees in India sent a letter to my employer in the U.S. falsely insinuating there was a conflict of interest with my being dually employed in India and in the U.S.

    ✍ The truth was I did not work for the company in India; I owned it outright.

    ✍ As a result, I spent the next several months providing my U.S. employer explanations to prove my innocence. I had to produce evidence to show that there was no conflict of interest, nor had I used any of the company's intellectual property in my venture. After thorough investigations by company lawyers and several HR representatives, the company found no evidence against me.

    ✍ But in the process, I lost my job.

I am not looking back and feeling sorry for myself over what happened in this unfortunate series of events, for it has strengthened my faith and character. God allows certain low points in our lives, so we can learn from them, especially when it comes to areas in which we are repeatedly resistant and ignore His warnings. Sometimes, trials are the only way he can get our attention.

Here are the dance lessons that I learned during

this journey:

Faith never grows in the garden of certainty.

It was a challenging year in which I faced several hurdles that tried my patience to the fullest. Another incident I would like to share with you left me feeling about as close as I ever want to come to hitting rock bottom.

One day, I took my daughter with me grocery shopping. Once we had selected all of our items, we headed to the checkout counter where I realized I didn't have enough money to pay for everything in the cart.

As the cashier rescanned every item one by one to remove the items I couldn't buy, it seemed all eyes were on me as my world turned in slow motion.

This episode had crushed my soul. At that very moment, I prayed that this would never happen to me again, or even to my enemies, especially to any dad. I was working but not consistently as a database consultant and trying to pay debts I accrued through my company in India.

As a husband, dad and head of the household, I didn't know how I could endure this type of hardship and not allow it to affect my wife and two children. I was very close to flipping out, and I wondered where God and my faith were in all this.

There seemed to be no answers to any of my prayers. It was like walking in a valley of darkness.

> ✍ God never leaves us nor forsakes us, and my faith continued to grow.

Hardships happen, but don't lose heart.

> ✍ God is our greatest provider and shows His providence all the time.

> ✍ Nothing is impossible for Him, and for over twelve months, I watched Him perform the impossible every day.

> ✍ Sometimes, we box God in by thinking He only performs miracles during times of hardship, rather than realize miracles happen all the time, but we fail to appreciate them.

> ✍ As Arnold Schwarzenegger once said, "Strength does not come from winning. Your struggles develop your strengths. When you go through hardships and decide not to surrender, that is strength."

The best dance step that I learned during this short journey of troubles and trials was that faith never grows in the garden of certainty.

I really didn't want to be like a weekend warrior, so I tried various avenues to increase my income and salvage the situation.

A friend in need is a friend indeed.

An unknown author once said, "When you look around and your world is crumbling, and when you think no one loves you, your best friend is the one to run to."

- ✍ I had several friends who were always there encouraging me to not give up. They were standing right by my side trying to help me reason through challenges to find viable solutions.

To this day, I still closely regard two of those friendships.

- ✍ One friend who played a key role in my financial recovery was Eric Standring. He is someone I can share intimate details with and not worry about being judged. He provided me emotional support.

- ✍ The other friend is Seetharaman. He's among the handful of people who came into my life for a season, making investments and leaving impressions that will last a lifetime.

✍ Words are not enough to explain the support Seetharaman has provided me. He never shied away when I was in trouble.

In summary, here is the life lesson I learned. Although hardships happen, don't ever lose hope and give up! Everything will turn out alright, and those who keep their hearts right will always have the last laugh.

✍ Ask God to give you the serenity to handle things that you cannot change.

Throughout life, we're not measured by how many people we love, but by how many people love us.

As a wise man once said, "Strength does not come from winning. Your struggles develop your strength. When you go through hardships and decide not to surrender, that is strength."

I am thankful God allowed Eric and Seetharaman to become a part of my life. Those are friendships I cherish the most.

Chapter 8

Things Happen for a Reason!
Life Spared

Are You Dancing in the Rain?

Things Happen for a Reason!
Life Spared

8

This chapter is dedicated to spiritual
leaders who instilled in me godly values
and principles.

John Milton, an English poet who ranks second only to Shakespeare, once said, "Gratitude bestows reverence, allowing us to encounter everyday epiphanies, those transcendent moments of awe that change forever how we experience life and the world."

Land where the milk and honey flow

Before leaving India to move to America, we were excited about heading to the world's most industrialized nation, a land of milk and honey. We were leaving a bustling commercial city in a nation with over a billion people and moving to a nation with over 200 million residents. As a citizen of a foreign country, I arrived in the states only to receive quite an unexpected introduction.

Like every other immigrant who comes to the United States of America, I came with lots of dreams of establishing my career and family here. This country is truly the land of the free and the home of the brave. As I walked out of the San Francisco Airport for the very first time, I felt a new sense of pride and accomplishment.

A transitioning period is always necessary whenever a foreigner moves to a new country. It requires adjusting to a new culture, understanding a new language and comprehending people's behaviors. It amazes me how quickly we adapted to the new world.

✍ There are lots of benefits people who grow up in this country simply take for granted, but those basic privileges must be earned by those moving here from other countries.

Similarly, if we take time to analyze our conflicts, we will see that there are lessons we should have learned from them. The incident I am about to share with you gave me a fresh perspective and appreciation for life.

Buying a computer

As I was happily settling in America, I was trying to learn additional skills at work to enlarge my career options, so I decided to buy a home computer.

At this point, I didn't have credit or debit cards, and the computer vendor wouldn't accept personal checks; so I withdrew fifteen $100 dollar bills from the bank and took a friend with me to pick up the computer. When I reached the store counter, the salesperson said the cost was $1,475, but that he didn't have $25 cash to give me change back.

So I left my money with him and walked down the block for about half an hour looking for someone who could give me change for a $100 dollar bill. Once I got it, I headed back to the store.

When I walked in the store, I noticed the salesman who took my cash was not there. Five completely different people were standing behind the counter, and one said, "Come on in. Your friend is here." As I walked toward the back, they pulled a gun out. Up until then, I had never seen a gun before in my life. At first, I thought they were joking, but soon I understood the seriousness of the situation and cooperated with them.

Apparently, while I was away looking for change, the store was taken over by a local gang from San Leandro, California. They came to steal everything in the store, but they were mainly interested in computer motherboards and CD ROMs, which were huge commodities they could easily sell.

After tying my hands and legs, they dragged me into a dark room. As I was lying on that hard, cold floor, I turned around and saw there were a few other guys lying on the floor in the same state as me. One of them was my friend and the other was the salesperson. They were both crying out not to be shot.

I was praying and reminding God to rescue me. I didn't hear roaring thunder or any audible voice from heaven, but gently I was reminded of this verse in the Bible. In Jesus' time, sparrows were sold for a very low price, two for a farthing (a small copper coin) but five for two farthings.

 It means one extra sparrow was free. It seems sparrows were of very little value in the eyes of men, and no one cared for them, but God cares for them because the Bible says, "not one of them is forgotten before God." Those words gave me comfort and strength to remain optimistic throughout that night.

During the next few hours, the gang stole all the merchandise in the entire shop. In spite of their threats, the salesman never let on that he had my $1,500 safely tucked in his pocket, so he never turned it over to them. As they were leaving, they shot a couple of bullets in the air but left the store without harming anyone. Just like we see in movies, we creatively found ways to untie ourselves and called the cops to come and rescue us.

The Birth of Proverbs226

That incident changed my perspective about life completely. For several months after that, the scene still lingered in my mind, and I prayed and asked God what I should do differently with my life. I knew my life was a gift from God, and He had allowed me to experience this senseless crime for a reason.

Initially, I was very angry with God and battled with Him every day. I wanted to leave the states and go back home to India. Somehow during that period of battling, my heart began to change. For the first time, instead of feeling anger toward the offenders, I began feeling sorry for them and their families, especially their children.

✍ When I researched information about an offender's life, what I found was their families and children are affected most by crimes they commit.

✍ Over 1.7 million American children have an incarcerated parent, which often results in negative school behavior and performance problems, as well as social stigma and shame.

Based on my research, I was amazed when I realized my experiencing that crime was not an isolated incident and that God would show me His plan through it. The statistics alarmed me greatly causing me to want to do something tangible to help the families of inmates, especially their children.

That prompted me to start Proverbs226, a non-profit agency to support inmates' children and rebuild their relationships with incarcerated parents. Plans for the project began resonating in my heart.

A series of life's events and my dad abandoning my mother helped me to clearly connect to and identify with inmates' children who have been abandoned by their parents. So my agency was not birthed out of sympathy, but out of empathy and my ability to relate.

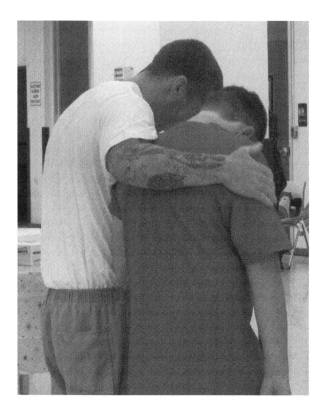

✍ Children are so vulnerable; the simplest question can cause them hurt and embarrassment, such as:

o "Where is your dad working?" Or
o "Can you bring your parents to school?"

When I see other children playing with their dads, it feels as if my soul has been cut with a sword. I am sure these children go through the same experience every single day, and they don't like to talk about the whereabouts of their parent(s) and definitely don't feel secure about their future.

A Danish proverb says, "The gem cannot be polished without friction, nor man be perfected without trials."

Every adversarial situation we face can certainly be turned into an opportunity to learn more about this journey we are traveling.

Chapter 9

Call to Action ~ Proverbs226

Are You Dancing in the Rain?

Call to Action ~ Proverbs226

9

This chapter is dedicated to all the precious children whose parents are incarcerated.

No one has yet realized the wealth of sympathy, the kindness and generosity hidden in the soul of a child. The effort of every true education should be to unlock that treasure. ~ **Emma Goldman**

Every child has a story. But for over 1.7 million American children who have a parent in prison, their story is often expressed in "silent tears." Each child has a unique story. All of them have compelling and powerful messages; however, by no means is this an attempt to cover every story. Allow the few stories presented below to touch your heart.

✎ At one point, I lived near Toronto, Canada, and during that time, I was once asked to take diapers to a mother who gave birth while in prison. What an environment in which to raise a child! Authorities allowed the mothers to care for their babies for the first few months after birth, which is why they needed help with diapers.

✎ Around the same time, in Waterloo, Ontario, I had the chance to meet with a 3-year-old toddler who cried and cried for several days after being separated from her mother who had been taken to prison.

What did these children do wrong to deserve this

level of hardship?

A song on young artist, Lindsay Logan's album, "Confessions of A Broken Heart," clearly portrays the inner cry of every one of these children. It pierced my heart sharply, to say the least. Here's a glimpse of her song, "Daughter to Father," which reflects this reality:

> Daughter to father, daughter to father...
> I don't know you, but I still want to.
> Daughter to father, daughter to father
> Tell me the truth, did you ever love me?
> Cause these are... these are
> the confessions of a broken heart.

Those lines describe the "silent tears" children of incarcerated parents deal with every day. "Did my dad or mom ever love me?"

✍ They are questioning why my mom or dad did not pick the pieces up for me. Children crave their parents' attention and love.

Another story is from an interaction with my

dear friend, Perry Tuttle. He played for Clemson and later in the NFL for the Atlanta Falcons and Tampa Bay Buccaneers. When I explained to him about the mission of Proverbs226 and what we are trying to do, this is what he said.

When he was a young boy, his dad was taken to prison. Even though Perry worked his way up in life, there was one thing that haunted him the most. In his heart, he wanted to find out whether his dad loved him or not.

As he grew up, he earned several credentials in his career (including fame, money and wealth), but he was not satisfied with any of them until one day, he received a letter from his dad.

For Perry, that was more than a love letter, and it gave him the completion that he was seeking.

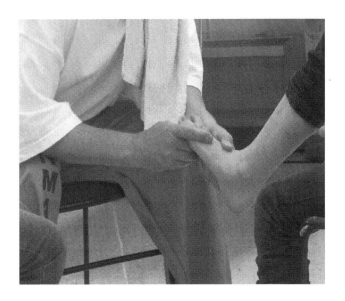

It doesn't matter whether a child is a newborn, a 3-year-old or an adult. All are assailed with the same question, "Did my dad ever love me?"

Lack of education

Children of incarcerated parents often exhibit poor behavior and performance problems in school.

✍ Approximately half of children with incarcerated parents are under 10 years of age. A very high percentage of these children will end up in prison.

✍ One of the causes for this alarming statistic is the lack of education. According to figures from the Children's Defense Fund, one out of every eight school children will not graduate. This means the population currently at risk of dropping out could be as many as 6,680,625 children.

✍ Let me give you some other statistics – 4,356 children are arrested every day in America. (Yes, this is every day! Multiply that by 365 days a year, and the annual figure is astounding!)

✍ Officials in several states know these stats very well and are building new prisons to create more beds to accommodate the children.

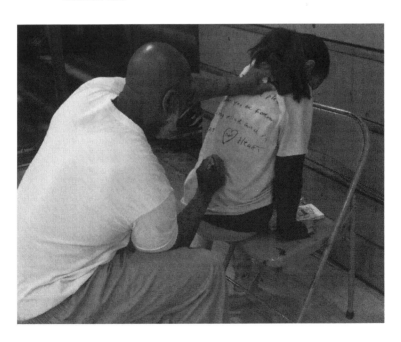

> ## OUR MISSION AT PROVERBS226:
>
> ## DEVELOP KIDS OF INCARCERATED PARENTS INTO COLLEGE GRADUATES

Those are the facts of life for many families in America. As you can see, one of the chief factors in their lives is "lack of education." Children who are at-risk have increased vulnerability in this area.

Call to action

Again, these stories are not meant to bring you just the shocking reality of what children are going through, but instead to call you to participate in helping them get over the hump.

We have created a platform for children and their families through a ministry called Proverbs226. The title of this effort is derived from a Bible verse that is found in the book of Proverbs written by King Solomon. It says, *"Train a child in the way he should go, and when he is old he will not turn from it." (Proverbs 22:6).*

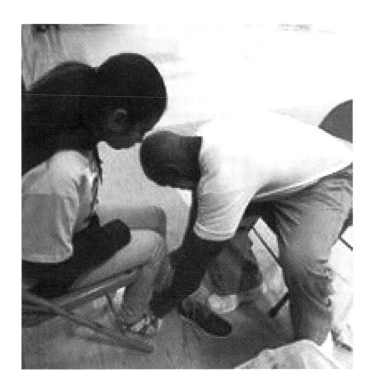

Before starting Proverbs226, I had a chance to meet and talk with several mothers who are taking care of children in the absence of their dads.

- ✍ One of them said, "I just need a break, juggling full-time work and full-time school myself."

- ✍ Another mom said, "My son's grades have fallen. I tried several things, like rewarding him for bringing them up and also punishments, none of which has worked. He needs tutoring, but I don't have enough resources to do that."

As you can see, their problem is not that they are giving up on their kids' education, but they do need extra help to get them over the hump.

Our vision can be condensed into two words, **"Generational Recidivism."** We want to start working with one prison at a time, so we can make a difference in their lives. Instead of creating a variety of programs, my team and I designed this project to focus on preventing kids from coming into the prison system.

What we are striving to do is change their identity, so the "cool thing" is not to jump over the moral fence to do the wrong thing, but instead to:

- ✍ Create meaningful relationships with the dad or mom who is incarcerated.

- ✍ Change "who they are" more than "what they do."

- ✍ Redefine their identity, and have them think about ethics and moral values, which will separate them from mediocrity.

- ✍ Raise the bar to high standards.

As Senator Hillary Clinton says in her book, *It Takes a Village*, we need to work as one team to change their paradigm. In order for this program to work, we need everyone working together.

    ✍ We need parents who are in prison to commit to making a difference in their children's lives.

    ✍ Caregivers (those responsible for taking care of the children) must create structure at home to help children stay in school and succeed.

✍ Educators or academic mentors can help children improve their grades in school and instruct them on how to excel in their educational pursuits.

✍ Finally, mentors, church or community leaders should assume the social responsibility of instilling in the children strong moral values and principles by which they should live.

Working together, we can make a difference in children's lives.

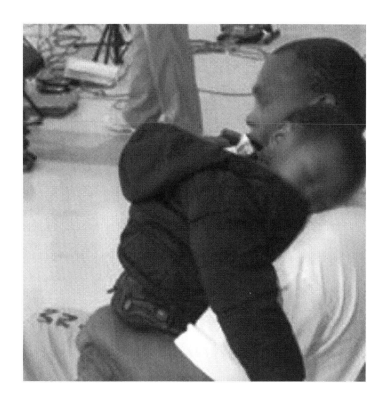

Even though we have created a general framework to work with the children, our goal is to prepare a customized "individual plan" for every child. The circumstances vary from child to child; therefore, we cannot implement one plan that will work the same way for all children.

As we walk through the vision for Proverbs226, I would like *for you to* consider the general plan outlined in this chapter as guiding principles and a framework to help fully equip our children for adult life.

Proverbs 226

Four steps are involved in equipping our children to succeed.

1. Engage

During the engagement process, we stress the importance of:

✐ Mending relationships between parents and children. We ask the dads to write a love letter to their children requesting forgiveness.

✎ Establishing a performance contract with each caregiver as a commitment that they will help the children in every way possible to stay in school.

✎ Parents interacting with their children in order to encourage them to stay in school.

2. Encourage

Mentoring and child advocacy:
Some children make an attempt to overcome their challenges but come to school carrying the weight of their burdens and family crises. We are bridging gaps between parents and children by:

♦ *Encouraging children to stay in school.*

♦ *Working with the school system and acting as a mediator between the children and the school as appropriate.*

♦ *Inspiring them with role models they can aspire to become like.*

3. Educate — Academic Mentoring

We will involve teachers and educators who will serve as academic mentors.

◆ They will invest their time in instructing the children.

◆ The caregivers will invest their time to be positive influences on the children, interacting with both child advocate mentors and academic mentors.

Our goal is to work with educators and the educational system to effectively help children to not only survive challenging times, but to achieve their goals as they are being fully equipped for their respective contributions to society.

4. Enable — Support scholarships for college

We will create platforms for the children to earn money for their college funds by:

♦ *Getting good grades in school, which earns them the necessary money for college.*

♦ *Actively participating in various events (such as talent shows) initiated by the organization to start earning their money.*

♦ As an organization, we are committed to supporting the children until they finish college or vocational school.

We are in search of mentors, academic mentors and event coordinators. If you are interested in being a part of the children's lives, we gladly welcome you to join us in serving them. The children may not have adequate school supplies; therefore, we provide supplies and backpacks, so they are ready for the start of school.

For more information on how you can be a part of Proverbs226, please visit us at: www.proverbs226.org or send us an e-mail to helpachild@proverbs226.org.

CONCLUSION

Life is like playing a keyboard, a guitar or some other musical instrument; it's not as important how well you play, but how playing makes you feel. The journey of life is not predictable, or we would make the right call regardless of circumstances. That's why we should not dwell so much on bad decisions that we rob ourselves of fulfillment.

Here are some of the key dancing attributes that I have learned in the course of my life:

✇ **Be the miracle.**

Every person craves a miracle, but they fail to understand God is not bored or eagerly waiting to wave a magic wand. Instead, He performs supernatural miracles for those who are tired and unable to get out of trouble. As Mahatma Gandhi once said, Do not look for a miracle, **be the miracle** (for someone who is in need).

✇ **Treat people with gentleness.**

People may not remember what you have said or done, but they will remember how you treated them. I came across several people who treated me well and played a significant role in giving my life an unexpected lift, and I was overwhelmed by it, so treat everyone with gentleness.

✍ Reconnect with your golden days.

When you get a chance, write down the good things that have happened in your life, so you can look back through the pages of your journey and remember the kindness you received from people crossing your path and thereby cherish their acquaintance.

We may need to use modern tools like search engines to look for old friends or elders whose company we once enjoyed, so we can reconnect with the golden days.

✍ Build resilience; there is an undeserved favor waiting for you.

I learned a significant lesson from looking at my life retrospectively. That has helped me to understand the undeserved favor that I received from God and from people around me.

David says in Psalms 34:19 (NIV), "The righteous person may have many troubles, but the LORD delivers him from them all;

He protects all his bones, not one of them
will be broken."

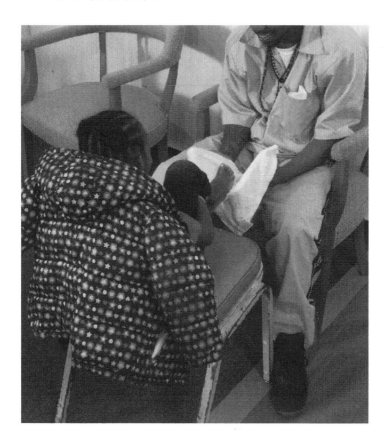

In life everyone has problems. Only the
intensity varies and how each of us handles
situations. That is what determines whether we live
lives in fullness. Faith is the substance that gives us
hope when the rubber meets the road. It confirms
the need for our reliance on supernatural power. In
other words, the deepest part of our souls seeks the
assurance of a safety zone. That's what the psalmist

is talking about.

Closing Thoughts

In this book, I have introduced a cast of characters who came into my life for a season and blessed me immensely. This is not a sad story, but a story of love and thanksgiving.

> ✍ The intent of this book is to allow you to let the characters of my story inspire you to recognize the goodness in people and the situations you come across.

> ✍ I have tried not to delete or skip the bad parts of my experience, since they have served as the cornerstone of the final product.

I do not have the recipe for every situation, but there are certain attributes and strategies we can learn from others' experiences that will help transform our lives from mediocre to good.

How can we have that passion burning within us, when life is filled with twists and turns? If you are going through a cycle of rough times, or when you feel like you are in the middle of the valley, continue to fight the good fight without losing heart, using your resources wisely.

We should **never allow sorrows to smile at us** by allowing our past to hinder us from moving forward. Instead, we must allow sorrows to become a positive foundation on which we can grow.

Remember, happiness is a state of mind, and the journey continues as we dance in the rain.

ABOUT THE AUTHOR

CYRIL PRABHU
Founder

Proverbs226
Ministries

Cyril Prabhu is a Senior Vice President for Bank of America where he has developed integrated business and technology strategies and solutions for nearly 25 years.

A certified Six Sigma Greenbelt, he has been presented the bank's Award of Excellence received by only the top 1% of associates. One of the teams he managed as chief designer has been credited with building the information pipeline for the bank's Global Commercial Banking.

Raised by a single mom in a nation where divorce was practically unheard of, Cyril overcame his hardships with the loving help of family, friends and perfect strangers. As he embraced circumstances over which he had no control, God caused favor to surround him and people rallied to his aid.

After relocating his family from India to California, a senseless crime jolted his image of the promised land. But rather than become bitter, he was inspired to establish Proverbs226 Ministries, a non-profit agency that steers inmates' children away from criminal activity and toward college. In addition to raising money for college scholarships, the agency provides moral, social and educational support for them to excel in life. It also hosts a variety of programs at prisons for the children and their parents.

Today, over 5,000 children participate in the program, which operates in 24 prisons in North Carolina, South Carolina, Texas and South Dakota, and it continues to grow.

Please visit our website to learn more about our program and find out how you can help: (www.proverbs226.org)

All proceeds from this book will go toward funding the college education of inmates' children.